O-TTPS FOR ICT PRODUCT INTEGRITY AN

A MANAGEMENT (

The Open Group Publications available from Van Haren Publishing

The TOGAF Series:
TOGAF® Version 9.1
TOGAF® Version 9.1 – A Pocket Guide
TOGAF® 9 Foundation Study Guide, 3rd Edition
TOGAF® 9 Certified Study Guide, 3rd Edition

The Open Group Series:
The IT4IT™ Reference Architecture, Version 2.0
IT4IT™ for Managing the Business of IT – A Management Guide
IT4IT™ Foundation Study Guide
The IT4IT™ Reference Architecture, Version 2.0 – A Pocket Guide
Cloud Computing for Business – The Open Group Guide
ArchiMate® 2.1 – A Pocket Guide
ArchiMate® 2.1 Specification
ArchiMate® 2 Certification – Study Guide
ArchiMate® 3.0 Specification

The Open Group Security Series:
O-TTPS - A Management Guide
Open Information Security Management Maturity Model (O-ISM3)
Open Enterprise Security Architecture (O-ESA)
Risk Management – The Open Group Guide
The Open FAIR™ Body of Knowledge – A Pocket Guide

All titles are available to purchase from:
www.opengroup.org
www.vanharen.net
and also many international and online distributors.

O-TTPS for ICT Product Integrity and Supply Chain Security

A Management Guide

Using the Open Trusted Technology Provider™ Standard
(O-TTPS) (ISO/IEC 20243:2015) and the Certification Program

Title:	O-TTPS for ICT Product Integrity and Supply Chain Security – A Management Guide
Series:	The Open Group Series
A Publication of:	The Open Group
Authors:	Sally Long and Members of The Open Group Trusted Technology Forum (OTTF)
Publisher:	Van Haren Publishing, Zaltbommel, www.vanharen.net
ISBN Hardcopy:	978 94 018 0092 1
ISBN eBook:	978 94 018 0093 8
ISBN ePub:	978 94 018 0094 5
Edition:	First edition, first impression, January 2017
Layout and Cover Design:	CO2 Premedia, Amersfoort – NL

O-TTPS for ICT Product Integrity and Supply Chain Security – A Management Guide
Document Number: G169
Published by The Open Group, January 2017
Comments relating to the material contained in this document may be submitted to:
The Open Group
Apex Plaza
Reading
Berkshire, RG1 1AX
United Kingdom
or by electronic mail to: ogpubs@opengroup.org

Contents

Preface

The Open Group

The Open Group is a global consortium that enables the achievement of business objectives through IT standards. With more than 500 member organizations, The Open Group has a diverse membership that spans all sectors of the IT community – customers, systems and solutions suppliers, tool vendors, integrators, and consultants, as well as academics and researchers – to:

- Capture, understand, and address current and emerging requirements, establish policies, and share best practices
- Facilitate interoperability, develop consensus, and evolve and integrate specifications and open source technologies
- Offer a comprehensive set of services to enhance the operational efficiency of consortia
- Operate the industry's premier certification service

Further information on The Open Group is available at www.opengroup.org.

The Open Group publishes a wide range of technical documentation, most of which is focused on development of Open Group Standards and Guides, but which also includes white papers, technical studies, certification and testing documentation, and business titles. Full details and a catalog are available at www.opengroup.org/bookstore.

Readers should note that updates – in the form of Corrigenda – may apply to any publication. This information is published at www.opengroup.org/corrigenda.

About The Open Group Trusted Technology Forum (OTTF) (the Forum)

The Forum, established under The Open Group in December 2010, is an organized collaboration among representatives from government, academia, and the IT industry. It develops and maintains the Open Trusted Technology Provider™ Standard – Mitigating Maliciously Tainted and Counterfeit Products (O-TTPS), also known as ISO/IEC 20243:2015. The mission of the Forum is to create and drive the adoption of the O-TTPS, the O-TTPS Certification Program, and other Forum deliverables.

For more information on the Forum, visit www.opengroup.org/subjectareas/trusted-technology.

About the O-TTPS Standard

The O-TTPS (and its equivalent ISO/IEC 20243:2015) is an open standard containing a set of requirements that when properly adhered to have been shown to enhance the security of the global supply chain and the integrity of commercial off-the-shelf (COTS) information and communication technology (ICT) products. It provides a set of guidelines, requirements, and recommendations that help assure against maliciously tainted and counterfeit products throughout the COTS ICT product life cycle, encompassing the following phases: design, sourcing, build, fulfillment, distribution, sustainment, and disposal, which includes the supply chain.

This Document

This Management Guide provides guidance on why a technology provider company should consider adopting O-TTPS and becoming certified; what they should understand about the Certification Program; and how they can best prepare for the process once they decide to pursue certification.

It is designed to offer guidance to managers – business managers, procurement managers, or program managers – who are considering becoming a certified Open Trusted Technology Provider™. Additionally, it provides an overview of the certification process, with pointers to the relevant supporting documents, offering a practical introduction to executives, managers, those involved directly in implementing the best practices defined in the Standard, and those who would provide the Evidence of Conformance to the best practice requirements for certification.

As the O-TTPS Certification Program is open to all constituents involved in a product's life cycle – from design through disposal – including those in the product's supply chain, this Management Guide should be of interest to all ICT customers as well as ICT providers (e.g., Original Equipment Manufacturers

(OEMs), Original Design Manufactures (ODMs), integrators, hardware or software component suppliers, value-add distributors, and resellers).

This Management Guide is structured as follows:

- Chapter 1 (Introduction) provides an executive summary, an overview of the threats and risks, some background information, a brief introduction to the Standard and the Certification Program, and a business rationale for getting certified as an Open Trusted Technology Provider.
- Chapter 2 (The Standard) gives an overview of the Standard and the categorization of the best practices that are required throughout the full product life cycle of a product. This chapter is an introduction to the structure of the Standard; the full set of requirements and recommendations in the Standard can be found in Appendix A.
- Chapter 3 (Organizing and Preparing for Certification) offers practical steps and best practices that will help an organization prepare and properly structure their approach for certification to best effect.
- Chapter 4 (The Certification Process) describes the certification processes. The information in this chapter should allow an organization to understand the basics of what is required to progress through the certification process. One of the first decisions the organization being certified should make is to decide on the type of assessment that best fits their business needs. The two options are: Self-Assessed and Third-Party Assessed.
- Chapter 5 (Self-Assessed Certification Process) covers the process for the Self-Assessed tier of the O-TTPS Certification Program in more detail.
- Chapter 6 (Third-Party Assessed Certification Process) covers the process for the Third-Party Assessed tier of the O-TTPS Certification Program in more detail.
- Chapter 7 (Summary of the Certification Steps) provides a list of the certification process steps as a summary, which can be found in more detail in the Certification Policy. Section 7.1 provides a summary of the steps for the Self-Assessed tier and Section 7.2 provides a summary of the steps for the Third-Party Assessed tier.
- Appendix A (O-TTPS Requirements) is a replica of the Terminology section (Section 1.4) of the Standard (i.e., O-TTPS Version 1.1, which is technically equivalent to ISO/IEC 20243:2015) that defines the prescriptive terms used in Chapter 4 of the Standard, which defines the requirements and recommendations for mitigating the risk of tainted and counterfeit products.

- Appendix B (Additional Resources) contains additional resources and references that provide useful information about the Forum, the O-TTPS, the O-TTPS Certification Program, and the Forum's other deliverables.

Conventions Used in this Management Guide

The following conventions are used throughout this Management Guide in order to help identify important information and avoid confusion over the intended meaning.

- The Standard
  Throughout this document when "the Standard" is used it should be interpreted as referring to both the O-TTPS and ISO/IEC 20243:2015, as they are technically equivalent. The Certification Program is applicable to both.
- Ellipsis (…)
  Indicates a continuation; such as an incomplete list of example items, or a continuation from preceding text.
- **Bold**
  Used to highlight specific terms.
- *Italics*
  Used for emphasis. May also refer to other external documents.

Trademarks

Acknowledgements

The Open Group gratefully acknowledges the following contributors in the development of this Management Guide:

- Past and present members of The Open Group Trusted Technology Forum (OTTF) for developing the Standard, the O-TTPS Certification Program, and the additional associated published documents. Those member companies include: atsec information security, Boeing, Booz Allen Hamilton, Carnegie Mellon University – Software Engineering Institute, Cisco Systems Inc., CyberCore Technologies, Dell, EMC, EWA-Canada, Huawei, Hewlett-Packard, IBM, Interos Solutions, Microsoft, MITRE, NASA, NTG, Oracle, Office of the Under Secretary of Defense for Acquisition/Technology and Logistics (OUSD AT&L), PCi Tec, Quinsigamond Community College, Strategic Communications, TaTa Consulting Services, and the US Department of Defense/CIO.
- The following contributors and reviewers:
  - Jon Amis, Dell Technologies
  - Erin Connor, EWA-Canada
  - Edna Conway, Cisco Systems Inc.
  - Terrie Diaz, Cisco Systems Inc.
  - Mike Lai, Microsoft Corporation
  - Fiona Pattinson, atsec information security corporation
  - Andy Purdy, Huawei Technologies USA
  - Dan Reddy, Quinsigamond Community College, previously of EMC Corporation
  - Andras Szakal, IBM Corporation
  - Joanne Woytek, NASA
  - Sally Long, The Open Group

Referenced Documents

The documents listed below are referenced in this Management Guide and can be accessed from the O-TTPS Certification website (http://ottps-cert.opengroup. org).

The published documents referenced below should be considered the official documents for the Standard and Certification Program, and take precedence over any content otherwise mentioned in this Management Guide.

- Assessment Procedures
- Certification Agreement
- Certification Package Document, including the Assessment Report
- Certification Policy
- Conformance Requirements
- Conformance Statement
- Conformance Statement Questionnaire
- Implementation Selection Criteria Application (ISCA) Document
- O-TTPS Recognized Assessor Agreement
- Open Trusted Technology Provider™ Standard (O-TTPS) (also now known as ISO/IEC 20243:2015)
- Trademark License Agreement

Chapter 1

Introduction

This document is intended for business managers, procurement managers, program managers, and other individuals who want to better understand product integrity and supply chain security information and communication technology (ICT) risks and how to protect their organization against those risks. It offers an approach toward mitigating those risks that has emerged through industry consensus, and which has been designed specifically for ICT providers.

This chapter provides an introduction to the adoption of the Open Trusted Technology Provider™ Standard – Mitigating the Risk of Maliciously Tainted and Counterfeit Products (O-TTPS), which was approved as ISO/IEC 20243:2015, and the O-TTPS Certification Program that helps assure conformance to the Standard. It also offers insight into the threats and risks that drive the need for this approach and the business rationale for adoption.

Topics addressed in this chapter include:
- Executive Summary
- Threats and Risks
- Background
- Introduction to the Standard and the O-TTPS Certification Program
- Business Rationale for Becoming an Open Trusted Technology Provider

Note: If the reader is already familiar with the cybersecurity and supply chain risks and the benefits to the O-TTPS approach and prefers to understand better what the Certification Program entails and how to prepare for the Program, then please refer to Chapter 2 through Chapter 7.

1.1   Executive Summary

In today's world, customers recognize their ever-increasing reliance on information and ICT to deliver mission-critical operations. They are cognizant and appreciative of the benefits of globalization in ICT, but are equally aware of the cybersecurity risks that come with worldwide development and global supply chains, risks from the effects of counterfeit or maliciously tainted products that could result in damage to their business environments or their mission-critical operations, and those users who depend on them.

Likewise, providers are keenly aware of the challenges related to building-in product integrity and supply chain security during the development, and throughout the life cycle, of their products. In today's global world, information technology supply chains depend on complex and inter-related networks of component suppliers across a wide range of global partners. Suppliers deliver hardware and software components to Original Equipment Manufacturers (OEMs) and Original Design Manufacturers (ODMs) who build products from the components, and in turn deliver products to customers directly or through a value-add reseller (who may add even more components) or to system integrators who integrate them with products from multiple providers at a customer site. This example of complexity leaves ample opportunity for malicious components to enter the supply chain and leave accessible exploits or vulnerabilities that can potentially be exploited.

The introduction of tainted products into the supply chain can pose significant risk to organizations because altered products can introduce the possibility of untracked malicious behavior. A compromised electronic component or piece of software that lies dormant and undetected within an organization could cause tremendous damage if activated remotely. Counterfeit products can also cause significant damage to customers and providers resulting in rogue functionality, failed or inferior products, or revenue and brand equity loss. As a result, customers now need assurances that they are buying from trusted technology providers who follow best practices with their own in-house secure development and engineering practices but also in securing their supply chains.

One approach to providing those assurances calls for leveraging the O-TTPS, an international standard for both establishing and maintaining product integrity and supply chain security, along with its accompanying Certification Program. The Standard is the first standard aimed at assuring *both* the integrity of COTS ICT products and the security of their supply chains. It is also the first standard with a Certification Program that specifies measurable conformance criteria for product integrity and supply chain security practices.

The Standard defines a set of best practices for COTS ICT providers to mitigate the risk of maliciously tainted and counterfeit components from being incorporated into any phase of a product's life cycle. This encompasses design, sourcing, build, fulfillment, distribution, sustainment, and disposal. The best practices apply to in-house development, outsourced development and manufacturing, and to global supply chains. It is not intended to satisfy all supply chain security and secure engineering questions, but it represents an important, foundational level of assurance based on proven and consistent practices.

The O-TTPS Certification Program, which is process-based and assures conformance to the best practices defined in the Standard, is applicable to all ICT providers in the chain: OEMS, ODMs, integrators, hardware and software component suppliers, value-add distributors, and resellers. When an applicant is certified for conformance, the applicant is granted the use of the Certification Logo and Trademark; the certification is acknowledged on a public registry; and the certified organization is identified as an Open Trusted Technology Provider, a mark that will resonate with technology customers and stakeholders.

When an organization is considering applying for certification, there are two major options to consider: the Scope of Certification and the tier of certification for which they will apply. An organization can choose between a Self-Assessed tier or a Third-Party Assessed tier.

Both tiers are backed by a warranty of conformance between The Open Group and the organization. Companies seeking certification need to understand the process and their obligations related to the Trademark License Agreement, the Certification Policy, and the Certification Agreement, in warranting conformance to the Standard in accordance with their chosen Scope of Certification.

The chief benefit of becoming an Open Trusted Technology Provider is that it helps providers "Build with Integrity" so that buyers can "Buy with Confidence". Achieving certification can ensure a level of protection that mitigates product and supply chain risks to customers while offering an ICT provider a means of demonstrating adherence to best practices to their stakeholders and customers, thus acting as a market differentiator. The technology providers who are certified and listed on the public registry assure customers acquiring COTS ICT that they are conformant to the best practices requirements defined in the Standard and will remain conformant, or they will be removed from the registry. By being certified as an Open Trusted Technology Provider a provider can more clearly articulate its security posture to its customers, who often contend with competing providers who assert that they meet a variety of inconsistent security requirements when responding to technology procurements.

Additionally, a provider could reduce its internal costs by adopting common requirements from the O-TTPS, which can be measured objectively. This can encourage companies to move away from custom requirements toward a consistent, recognized industry baseline.

This Management Guide highlights the risks associated with a global economy and global supply chains and the benefits for addressing those risks through international standards and vendor-neutral conformance programs. It offers additional details on the Standard and how to prepare for certification.

1.2   Threats and Risks

This section provides an introduction to some of the threats that drive the need for mitigating the risk of taint and counterfeit components from ICT products.

1.2.1   Risk Lies in Complexity, Including the Global Economy

Most thoughtful and sophisticated ICT customers and providers manage the security of their organizations based on risk. They consider the risk based on the threats, the vulnerabilities, the potential impact of cyber attacks, the likelihood of them occurring, and the best methods to manage those risks. As cyber attacks increase in sophistication, stealth, and severity, governments and larger enterprises have begun to take a more comprehensive and insistent view of the criticality of risk management and product assurance. Unfortunately, we are exposed to cyber attacks with increasing regularity. In addition to enhancing information security by improving security practices across the enterprise, governments and enterprises have begun including in their assessment of risk the risk from suppliers and third-party providers, which is directly related to the practices IT providers use to ensure the security and protect the integrity of their products as they move through the complex global supply chain. It is often not economically feasible – nor does it in any way eliminate supplier risk – to simply restrict ICT acquisition based on geographical preferences. The key from a risk management perspective is to examine these providers' global organizational practices as components and products are developed, manufactured, and delivered throughout the world regardless of country of origin or destination.

1.2.2 Maliciously Tainted and Counterfeit Components

Maliciously tainted products pose significant security risks. For example, they could allow unauthorized access to sensitive corporate data, including potential theft of intellectual property, or allow attackers to take control of the organization's cyber assets for any number of malicious purposes. Normal functional testing is often ineffective in uncovering sophisticated exploits. One risk is that high quality, malicious software or malware-enabled counterfeit components may lie dormant and undetected for long periods until the attacker chooses to launch the malevolent feature.

Like maliciously tainted components, counterfeit products can also cause significant damage to customers and providers resulting in rogue functionality, failed or inferior products, revenue and brand equity loss, compromised data, and the disclosure or theft of intellectual property. With the complex make up of today's global supply chain, comes the risk of more sophisticated maliciously tainted or high quality counterfeit parts making their way into operational environments. Thus, a compromised or maliciously designed electronic component or piece of software, with otherwise normal functionality, could cause tremendous damage when activated by a triggering event, or under conditions imposed by the attacker.

A risk-based approach to acquisition of ICT will not perfectly eliminate risk but will allow the enterprise to manage it pursuant to the organization's risk posture. The threats of exploitation of vulnerabilities in software, and compromising hardware through counterfeits, can be mitigated by technology providers responsibly following recognized, independently confirmed best practices. This means that it is imperative for buyers of ICT to make their acquisitions from providers who follow secure development and engineering practices in-house while developing their own products, but who also follow best practices to secure their supply chains.

Government and critical infrastructure organizations have expressed interest in understanding how providers manage the risks inherent in globalized product development and manufacturing and are asking the following questions:

- How can ICT customers and providers manage this risk in an efficient and cost-effective manner?
- What are the foundational practices that should be required to offer assurance as a baseline?
- Where can customers find an international standard that has been vetted as practical and effective?
- Is there a standard that has measurable conformance criteria to mitigate cyber and technology development and supply chain security risks?

The Standard and the O-TTPS Certification Program discussed in this Management Guide provide the answer to some of those important questions.

1.3   Background

For some time customers, including governments, have been moving away from building their own customized systems and products for higher assurance, and are instead using more COTS ICT products, typically because they are better, less expensive, widely available, more reliable, and fit for necessary purposes. This naturally introduces a greater risk of maliciously tainted or counterfeit elements than when development and production are done in-house.

This paradigm shift led to some initial roundtable discussions with government and industry to explore what it would take to be able to identify trusted technology providers and their COTS ICT products. These discussions spawned the creation of an *ad hoc* working group, which in 2010 transitioned to oversight by The Open Group as The Open Group Trusted Technology Forum (OTTF) (the Forum). The development of the Standard and Certification Program is the result of work by the Forum, which is an organized collaboration among representatives from government, academia, and the IT industry. The Forum members, which include representatives from numerous industry leaders – that both cooperate and compete – set out to develop a systematic approach to address the risks articulated above. The Forum worked for several years to identify and share their effective practices for product integrity, product development, and supply chain security. Through a consensus process informed by these experiences and discussions, the Forum members identified an agreed set of best practices, which were standardized using The Open Group consensus review process. This produced a method of identifying these fundamental practices and producing a means of measuring them that would scale on a global basis.

The resulting standard was originally published as the O-TTPS Version 1.0 in April 2013, and Version 1.1 was published in July 2014. Version 1.1 was then adopted as an ISO/IEC standard in September 2015 as ISO/IEC 20243:2015. This further extended the global reach of what the Forum members had achieved given the prominence of ISO/IEC standards. The Open Group also developed the O-TTPS Certification Program, which was launched in January 2014 and provides for assessment and recognition of any technology provider organization that conforms to the Standard. This benefits both the supplier and buyer communities by giving suppliers accepted industry-common targets to build into their processes, and enabling buyers to more easily identify providers and products that meet proven, secure, trusted development, manufacturing, and supply chain criteria.

The Forum is a global initiative that invites industry, government, and other interested participants to work together to evolve the Standard, the O-TTPS Certification Program, and other deliverables. For more information on the Forum, including a link to OTTF publications, visit www.opengroup.org/subjectareas/trusted-technology.

1.4 Introduction to the Standard and the O-TTPS Certification Program

This section provides an introduction to the Open Trusted Technology Provider™ Standard (O-TTPS), a standard of The Open Group approved as ISO/IEC 20243:2015, and to the O-TTPS Certification Program.

The requirements within the Standard provide best practices for product integrity and supply chain security to be followed throughout the product life cycle, from design through disposal. The best practices are applicable to providers of COTS ICT: OEMs, ODMs, hardware and software component suppliers, value-add resellers, and distributors.

The O-TTPS Version 1.1 is available free-of-charge from The Open Group Bookstore at: www.opengroup.org/bookstore/catalog/c147.htm.

The ISO/IEC 20243:2015 standard is available from the ISO website for a fee at: www.iso.org/iso/home/store/catalogue_tc/catalogue_detail.htm?csnumber=67394.

Note: The two standards are technically equivalent. Therefore, in this document references to the O-TTPS should be taken to also refer to ISO/IEC 20243:2015, and in other instances we use the term "the Standard" to indicate either. However, the Certification Program, which provides certification by The Open Group for conformance to either version of the standard, is referred to as the O-TTPS Certification Program. Similarly, certification-related documents will include the O-TTPS name in the reference.

The O-TTPS Certification Program is publicly available and open to all providers who conform to the Standard. The O-TTPS Certification Program documents include policies, conformance criteria, assessment procedures, a trademark license to use the certification mark, and a public registry for any Open Trusted Technology Provider who has been certified through the Program. More details of the O-TTPS Certification Program can be found at: http://ottps-cert.opengroup.org.

When an organization is considering applying for certification, there are two major options to consider:

1. The Scope of Certification; an organization can choose to be certified for their product life cycle practices for a particular scope. The scope can be the entire organization, a business unit, a product line, or one or more individual products.
2. The tier of certification for which they will apply; an organization can choose between a Self-Assessed certification or the Third-Party Assessed certification.

Both tiers are backed by a warranty of conformance between The Open Group and the organization. Companies seeking certification need to understand the process and their obligations related to the Trademark License Agreement, the Certification Policy, and the Certification Agreement, in warranting conformance to the Standard in accordance with their chosen Scope of Certification. In the warranty, the organization claims that to the best of their knowledge they are conformant to the Standard within their Scope of Certification and that they will remain conformant throughout the certification period (three years) or they will be removed from the public registry – please see the Certification Policy and Certification Agreement for the specific details on the warranty.

Chapter 2 and Appendix A of this Management Guide provide further details on the Standard. Chapter 3 through Chapter 7 of this Management Guide provide guidance on the O-TTPS Certification Program.

1.5   Business Rationale for Becoming an Open Trusted Technology Provider

The Standard and O-TTPS Certification Program for product integrity and supply chain security are important steps in the continued battle to secure ICT products and protect the environments in which they operate. Adhering to relevant international standards and demonstrating conformance is a powerful tool for global technology providers and component suppliers. This can be leveraged to combat cyber attacks on critical infrastructure, governments, business enterprises, and connected homes. Adoption and certification is the first step in mitigating this challenge.

There are several compelling business reasons why a technology provider should pursue certification as an Open Trusted Technology Provider. Decision-makers should consider the potential outcomes of the certification process and the value and distinction of having their organization certified.

Good companies are focused on their customers. They wish to demonstrate their added value and to certainly prevent negative consequences to their customers. Being certified as an Open Trusted Technology Provider enables a technology provider to better articulate their security posture to their customers, and how they meet customer procurement requirements.

In evaluating the business case for certification, a technology provider's leadership should weigh the potential resource investments against benefits that may flow from certification. Some benefits include:

- Reduced risk of counterfeit and maliciously tainted components in ICT products that could impact customers
- Competitive edge in earning and retaining business through a demonstrated security achievement

- Visibility to upstream and downstream risk which could both affect its brand and customer engagement

With the achievement of conforming to an international standard, providers can go beyond dialog with customers to offer measurable results. The transparent criteria of the Standard and objective assessments of the O-TTPS Certification Program allow all constituents to collectively address this key security challenge. The Standard does so in a vendor and geographically-neutral manner across the ICT ecosystem. Many good organizations that are addressing secure engineering and supply chain security have started to build a track record through their practices. Often they are self-determined security practices; sometimes they are shared with other companies.

The effort to tie a single company's practices to an international standard that can be practically measured for conformance to both secure engineering and supply chain security can be a challenge, but that effort of voluntary adoption and internal accountability to the Standard will improve an organization's security practices. Conducting surveys of all of an ICT provider's suppliers takes a significant amount of sustained effort given the complexity noted above. However, on the other-hand, with measureable certification to the Standard an ICT provider and their suppliers can independently establish a fundamental achievement and offer a common baseline level of assurance to their customers and their business partners. Certification demonstrates that many of a provider's key practices reach down and across a provider's supply chain. Customers may still want to build on that foundation in a quest for high assurance, but the customers in that case start with an understanding that the fundamentals are in place. Thus, providers investing in and attaining these practices and processes would gain a deserved market differentiation.

Chapter 2

The Standard

The Standard is described in terms of the provider's product life cycle. The collection of provider best practices contained in the Standard are those that are considered best capable of influencing and governing the integrity of a COTS ICT product from its inception to proper disposal at end-of-life. These provider practices are divided into two basic categories of product life cycle activities: technology development and supply chain security, as described below:

- The provider's technology development activities for a COTS ICT product are mostly under the provider's in-house supervision in how they are executed. The methodology areas that are most relevant to assuring against tainted and counterfeit products are:
  - Product Development/Engineering methods
  - Secure Development/Engineering methods
- The provider's supply chain security activities focus on best practices where the provider must interact with third parties who produce their agreed contribution with respect to the product's life cycle. Here, the provider's best practices often control the point of intersection with the outside supplier through control points that may include inspection, verification, and contracts.

While these categories are useful as an organizing construct, they are not absolute distinctions; for example, one product may be handled by the provider's own organization exclusively, while another product's life cycle could involve many aspects being handled in conjunction with a variety of third parties as governed by the provider. These two major categories of the product life cycle are depicted in Figure 1:

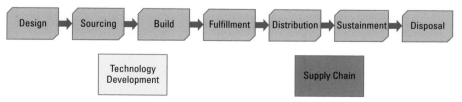

Figure 1: Product Life Cycle – Categories and Activities

The Standard includes the prescriptive requirements and recommendations for these major categories and activities. The requirements are focused on the two identified threats (i.e., taint and counterfeit). Some of the requirements are highly correlated to the specific threats; others are more foundational but considered essential.

The Standard and the Assessment Procedures document, which is also public and offers guidelines on the types of evidence that indicate conformance to each requirement in the Standard, are structured along the lines of these three major categories and the naming convention is illustrated below:
- PD: Product Development/Engineering Method
- SD: Secure Development/Engineering Method
- SC: Supply Chain Security

The following sections illustrate how the Standard is structured and provides a sample related to each of the major categories. Appendix A of this Management Guide provides the complete set of attributes, requirements, and recommendations from the Standard.

2.1   Technology Development

2.1.1   PD: Product Development/Engineering Method

The following section contains examples of the best practice requirements and recommendations primarily associated with the Technology Development category of activities relating to the product life cycle.

2.1.1.1   PD_DES: Software/Firmware/Hardware Design Process

Attribute Definition
A formal process exists that defines and documents how requirements are translated into a product design.

Requirements
Note: While these tables are listed under "Requirements" in the Standard, at the current writing of this standard, only the mandatory requirements (i.e., "shall" statements) are considered mandatory and only the "shall" statements are

required to be assessed for conformance through the Certification Program. The "should" statements are considered recommendations.

PD_DES.01	A process shall exist that assures the requirements are addressed in the design.
PD_DES.02	Product requirements shall be documented.
PD_DES.03	Product requirements should be tracked as part of the design process.

2.1.2   SE: Secure Development/Engineering Method

2.1.2.1   SE_TAM: Threat Analysis and Mitigation

Attribute Definition
Threat analysis and mitigation identify a set of potential attacks on a particular product or system and describe how those attacks might be perpetrated and the best methods of preventing or mitigating potential attacks.

Requirements

SE_TAM.01	Product architecture and design shall be assessed against potential attacks to gain an understanding of the threat landscape.
SE_TAM.02	Threat mitigation strategies for tainted and counterfeit products shall be implemented as part of product development.
SE_TAM.03	Threat analysis shall be used as input to the creation of test plans and cases.

2.2   Supply Chain Security

2.2.1   SC: Supply Chain Security
The following section contains an example of the best practice requirements and recommendations primarily associated with the Supply Chain Security category of activities relating to the product life cycle.

2.2.1.1 SC_RSM: Risk Management

Attribute Definition
The management of supply chain risk around tainted and counterfeit components and products includes the identification, assessment, prioritization, and mitigation of corresponding business, technical, and operational risks.

Requirements

SC_RSM.01	Changes to the threat landscape should be monitored by periodically reviewing industry security alerts/bulletins.
SC_RSM.02	Supply chain risk identification, assessment, prioritization, and mitigation shall be conducted.
SC_RSM.03	The output of risk identification, assessment, and prioritization shall be addressed by a mitigation plan, which shall be documented.
SC_RSM.04	The output of risk identification, assessment, and prioritization shall be addressed by a mitigation plan, which shall be followed routinely.
SC_RSM.05	The mitigation plan should be reviewed periodically by practitioners, including management, and revised as appropriate.
SC_RSM.06	Supply chain risk management training shall be incorporated in a provider's organizational training plan, which shall be reviewed periodically and updated as appropriate.

Chapter 3

Organizing and Preparing for Certification

In this chapter we focus on the steps and best practices that will help an organization prepare and properly structure their approach for certification to best effect. Proper preparation will pay significant dividends, especially leading up to engaging a certification lab partner or establishing an internal project group. Customizing this guidance to your organizational needs is also an essential step toward effective preparation as no two organizations are ever the same. The guidance provided here has been sourced from organizations that have already successfully navigated the O-TTPS Certification Program or similar.

3.1 Preparing for Certification

3.1.1 Organizational Impact

Here we outline steps to ensure effective leadership and communication of the value of certification and steps that should be considered in order to properly structure the certification process to extract the desired Return on Investment (ROI) from the certification itself.

Step 1: Solicit Executive Sponsorship
Because this certification is an assessment of risk against the organization's ability to execute mitigation practices, it is imperative that a leader with the proper span of control owns the initiative and process of certification. It may well be a partnership between several executives or senior leaders. Together they must agree to drive the focus, reviews, and funding from start to finish. This is normally a leader or set of leaders who have some involvement in managing the supply chain or are directly responsible for managing the development or engineering processes.

Step 2: Understand the Certification Process
Assign someone to research and understand the certification process so they can better inform the executives and senior leaders. This person should become

familiar with the process through the O-TTPS Certification Program website by reading and understanding all of the supporting documents and what each of the steps in the process entail. This Management Guide, in particular Chapters 4, 5, and 6, provide a good overview, but the home page, or the Getting Started web page at http://ottps-cert.opengroup.org, is the definitive place to go for all the information they will need. If there are questions on the process they should either contact The Open Group Certification Authority via the O-TTPS Certification website (http://ottps-cert.opengroup.org) for clarification on the process, or consult with one of the O-TTPS Recognized Assessors[1] who will also understand what is required, especially as it relates to steps in the assessment process. The O-TTPS Recognized Assessor registry can be found here: http://ottps-cert.opengroup.org/recognized-assessors.

Step 3: Drive Cross-Organizational Communication

Effective communication is the best indicator of success. Executive sponsors must effectively communicate across the organization their intent to embrace the Standard and attain certification. This includes realization of the impact and ROI these practices will bring to the organization. Garnishing support for compliance without fully understanding the implication of the practices defined by the Standard may cause unnecessary delays and increase project risk.

Explaining how the use of the best practices will help increase agility, reduce risk, and raise the organization's credibility are all valid ways of explaining why it is worth the effort and how it will provide a ROI.

Step 4: Establish a Project

Below are some essential elements in framing a project:

- Assign a project leader/manager who will be responsible for the day-to-day execution of the certification process and are empowered to lead remediation of any identified gaps.
- Establish a project cadence by establishing a weekly review to discuss challenges and resolve issues. Ensure they are providing the organization sponsors with frequent updates and externalizing challenges to stakeholders.

---

[1] Hereafter, O-TTPS Recognized Assessor (company) may also be called Recognized Assessor or simply Assessor.

- Outline and communicate the steps or journey map that will define the overall process. This plan should be communicated and agreed by all parties and stakeholders involved.

Step 5: Manage the Assets
A centralized collaboration and document management hub (use your tool of choice) will be necessary to manage assets, document communications, and store assets associated with the certification process. It is important that version control and configuration management be part of this effort. This includes properly securing all information associated with implementation or assessment as it is likely to contain confidential, sensitive information.

3.1.2   Mapping Internal Policies and Practices to the Standard
Certification is not simply the process of filling out forms and responding to documentation requests. The organization must map existing internal policies and practices to the Standard's conformance criteria and provide evidence of that conformance. Remember there is no specific "right" way for an organization to craft their policies or their practices; this is about looking to see if conforming practices are in place. This is best done before starting the formal certification process and serves to identify any gaps before starting a formal certification project. Below are some guidelines for determining readiness for certification.

- Review internal policies with execution teams to determine the level of internal adoption of the organization's internal policies that are congruent with the conformance criteria. Put another way – make sure you are following your own pertinent internal policies first. This will eliminate surprises.
- Use the internal review process to help conduct a gap analysis and adjust internal policies and practices that may be in conflict. Again, the executive sponsor will play a key role by ensuring this activity gets the proper resource allocation.
- Use other external certification collateral as reference resources that may support and augment the Evidence of Conformance:
  - Collect this information into categories mapped to risk mitigation practices and conformance criteria. Ensure these are stored in the central collaboration hub used for this project.
  - Map external certification requirements to the Standard and identify evidence used in previous evaluations – for example, industry assessments like FedRamp, Common Criteria, or ISO27K assessments – that may be applicable.

3.1.3   Closing Gaps in Conformance

It is unrealistic to believe that an Assessor will not find gaps or at least perceived gaps. Instead, build and prepare your team in a way that will focus them on addressing and closing identified gaps as quickly as possible. Below are some guidelines on identifying and closing the gaps:

- Review gap analysis with executive sponsors, rank perceived or identified gaps according to effort, and categorize as low, medium, or high. Then assign separate resources to focus on each category of prioritized gaps if practical. This will allow the organization to remediate as many gaps as possible in the shortest possible period of time. Remember to leverage the rest of this Management Guide focused on this topic.
- Some gaps will result in cure plans that may require changes to policy, practices, or tools. It is best to catch these gaps prior to the start of the certification assessment. In many cases gap remediation can be conducted in parallel while the certification assessment continues.
- Gather and consolidate in your collaboration or content hub as much Evidence of Conformance as possible. This includes activities related to enablement, training, and reports that demonstrate the evidence supports the conformance criteria. Put these all in the common repository along with a description of the asset and how it maps to the conformance criteria. This will help you and the Assessors understand the purpose of the asset.
- Ensure your organization understands that the conformance criteria are the way in which we measure that an organization is conformant to the best practices defined in the Standard. The current conformance criteria can be found in the Conformance Requirements Document, which at the writing of this document, is that all mandatory requirements ("shall" requirements as defined in Chapter 4 of the Standard) must be met. These can also be found in Appendix A of this Management Guide. The types of evidence required to demonstrate conformance are documented in the Assessment Procedures, which can be found on the Getting Started web page at http://ottps-cert.opengroup.org in the left-hand navigation bar.

3.1.4   Preparing for the Assessment

As noted in more detail in Chapter 4 of this Management Guide, there are two certification tier options: Self-Assessed and Third-Party Assessed. The following sections contain preparation guidelines for each option.

3.1.4.1 Self-Assessed Tier
If your organization is considering the Self-Assessed tier, then the following guidelines may be helpful. Please note that in general the guidelines in Section 3.1.1 through Section 3.1.3 of this chapter are applicable to both tiers.
- Your organization will need to assign an assessment team to essentially act in the role of the lab assessor. They will be required to behave in a similar manor to a third-party testing laboratory.
- Separate the assessment team from the project office.
- It may be advantageous to contract with an evaluation lab, such as an O-TTPS Recognized Assessor, to help with the self-assessment.
- Don't make the team responsible for conducting the self-assessment synonymous with the project team responsible for oversight and remediation.
- Your organization will need to determine its Scope of Certification. Considerations for determining the scope are detailed further in Section 3.1.4 of this chapter and in Chapter 5 of this Management Guide.
- All of the requirements in the Standard are applicable to both the Self-Assessed and the Third-Party Assessed tiers.

3.1.4.2 Third-Party Assessed Tier
If your organization is considering the Third-Party Assessed tier, then the following guidelines may be helpful. Please note that in general the guidelines in Section 3.1.1 through Section 3.1.3 of this chapter are applicable to both tiers.

Partnering with an O-TTPS Recognized Lab Assessment Organization
Finding the right lab assessment partner is essential to success. Most importantly, you are required to choose an Assessor from the O-TTPS Recognized Assessor registry, which can be found here: http://ottps-cert.opengroup.org/recognized-assessors. Additionally, each O-TTPS Recognized Assessor has slightly different business and assessment practices. Many lab assessment organizations come prepared with their own tools and consulting practices. You need to make sure the lab you select fits your organizational personality and business practices.

That does not mean they are simply going to rubber stamp your assessment. Just as in any business relationship you have to do your part. But finding an assessment lab that matches your organization's personality is important.

Some factors to consider:
- Don't forget that contracting with a new partner may require some work to get them on your company's approved contracting list.
- Find an assessment lab that aligns with the size and complexity of your organization. Validate that they have the right expertise. Ask about what value-add the lab may bring to your assessment; for example, tools or frameworks that can help structure and better organize your organization's assessment.

Some steps to take in progressing the partnership:
- Conduct an initial meeting with a potential lab (from the O-TTPS Recognized Assessor registry) and establish a relationship that includes understanding:
  – Their fee structure and the process by which they manage assessments
  – The potential lab partner's level of expertise – determine if they understand the Standard, supply chain security, and secure engineering practices
  – Their familiarity with the tools and practices used by your organization
  – The tools they have developed to help them automate their assessment – this will help you as well
- Negotiate a contract that will benefit both parties – and lock down any additional fees up-front. Avoid having to renegotiate the contract in the middle of an assessment. The fees will to a large extent be based on your Scope of Certification – see Chapter 5 of this Management Guide.
- Hiring a pre-assessment consultant to identify and help close gaps helps avoid any surprises and may help you make a case for why you are conformant in those cases where the Assessor identifies potential gaps. If this is not practical, then conduct your own internal assessment. Your certification lab cannot be under contract for consulting while simultaneously conducting the certification assessment.
- Review the O-TTPS Recognized Assessor Agreement, accessible from the O-TTPS Certification website, so that your organization understands the process and practices the Assessor is required to conduct by the Certification Authority. The Certification Authority is The Open Group staff assigned to the certification operations and management role for the O-TTPS Certification Program.

Determine and Document your Scope of Certification

The Scope of Certification is important because, ultimately, by signing the Certification Agreement, your organization is warranting that they are conformant to the mandatory requirements in the Standard throughout the Scope of Certification. Below are some factors to consider when choosing your Scope of Certification:

- If this is your initial assessment, then start with the portion of your organization that your executive sponsor believes has the best chance of meeting the Conformance Requirements with little or no remediation. This will affect your decision process for determining the Scope of Certification – i.e., which products and teams will be assessed against the criteria and how much of your organization will be listed as conformant.

- If you have a broad Scope of Certification with many products, then you need to make sure that your Implementation Selection Criteria Application (ISCA) – see Chapter 6 of this Management Guide – effectively represents the diversity of your scope.

- Depending on the size and complexity of the organization, you may not want to evaluate all of your organization at once. Consider segmenting your organization into multiple assessments. This will ensure that if one segment of the business needs significant remediation it does not hold up the assessment of other portions of the organization.

Note: There are additional details on the Scope of Certification in Chapter 5 and Chapter 6 of this Management Guide.

Kick Off Meetings and Initial Assessments

When you have determined the Scope of Certification, conduct a kick-off meeting that includes representatives from all of the product or program units that are being considered for certification. The following factors should be considered:

- Communicate their need to support the Assessor in their questions and provide assets to the certification team in a timely manner – not communicating effectively will increase the difficulty and cost of the certification.

- Gather as much information as feasible from the teams associated with the Scope of Certification before the assessment formally begins – this will increase the velocity and reduce the cost of the assessment.

- Initial assessments should begin with a face-to-face meeting between you and the assessment lab – this will help with communication and collaboration.

Closing Gaps Identified by the Assessor

Expect that the Assessor will identify the need for additional evidence, documentation, or further explanation. In order to address these, it is helpful to:

- Establish a bi-weekly meeting with the Assessor to communicate progress, fulfill information requests, and discuss any issues.
- Establish a project team that is dedicated to the assessment once it begins. This implies it will be the job of some number of staff until complete. Remember, the faster you are able to action Assessor requests, and work with the affected teams, the lower the assessment costs and the faster you will achieve certification.

Communicating the Assessment Review

The wrap-up of the assessment is important to the team. Some things to remember when bringing closure to the process:

- Hopefully your organization will successfully complete the assessment, become certified, and have positive news to communicate externally. But it's important that folks understand that if your organization signs the Trademark License Agreement, they are agreeing to continued support of the practices and are legally bound to do so until you no longer agree to the terms.
- A successful certification assessment is a good time to celebrate the success of the organization and embark on the next level of adoption across those teams that were not considered in earlier certifications. This is also a great opportunity to help other parts of the organization realize that certification is an achievable effort that provides tangible business value.
- All is not lost if the initial assessment is not positive. This is a time for reflection and internal assessment and you still need to communicate the results from a positive perspective; focusing on what your organization must do to adopt these industry best practices – in many cases it is a matter of automation and formalization or organizational policies to ensure their enforcement.

Chapter 4

The Certification Process

The information in this chapter describes the certification processes, which are also described in the O-TTPS Certification Policy and on the Getting Started web page at http://ottps-cert.opengroup.org of the O-TTPS Certification website. The information in this chapter should allow an organization to understand the basics of what is required to progress through the certification process.

One of the first decisions the organization being certified should make is to decide on the type of assessment that best fits their business needs. The two options are:

- Self-Assessed
- Third-Party Assessed

In order to make that decision, an organization should understand the big picture of what to expect throughout their chosen assessment tier. More detailed information can be found as follows:

- For the Self-Assessed certification tier, Chapter 5 is applicable.
- For the Third-Party Assessed certification tier, Chapter 6 is applicable.

Preparation for either tier requires the following: a basic knowledge of the Standard and its requirements (which are found in Appendix A of this Management Guide), review of the supporting certification documents, and an understanding of the attestations and warranties that the organization must make in connection with this type of certification.

The relevant documents that are *common to both* the Self-Assessed and the Third-Party Assessed approaches are listed in Table 1.

Note: The Certification Authority, referred to throughout this Management Guide and in Table 1 is the organization that manages the day-to-day operations of the O-TTPS Certification Program in accordance with Certification Policy.

Authorized staff of The Open Group serve as the Certification Authority for the
O-TTPS Certification Program.

Table 1: Supporting Certification Documents (for Self-Assessed and Third-Party Assessed Tiers)

Documents	Definition	Major Relevance
Certification Agreement	The agreement between the organization and the Certification Authority that defines the certification service to be provided and contains the legal commitment by the organization to the conditions of the O-TTPS Certification Program.	By signing this Agreement, the organization warrants and represents to the Certification Authority that, to the best of the organization's knowledge, for the chosen Scope of Certification, the organization meets the Conformance Requirements at the time of certification and that, after achieving certification, will continue to meet the Conformance Requirements throughout the duration of certification, in accordance with the Certification Policy.
Conformance Requirements	The O-TTPS requirements that an organization must meet in order to demonstrate conformance to the Standard. Those requirements are declared in the Conformance Requirements document.	At the time of the writing of this document, for Version 1.1 of the Standard, an organization must meet all of the mandatory ("shall") requirements in Chapter 4 of the Standard; accordingly, it is not necessary that the organization also meet the optional ("should") requirements.

Documents	Definition	Major Relevance
Certification Policy	The Certification Policy and its associated documents govern the operation of the O-TTPS Certification Program. This policy defines what can be certified, what it means to be certified, and the process for achieving and maintaining certification. This policy also defines the obligations of organizations, including a requirement that within a declared Scope of Certification it meets the Conformance Requirements, which include conformance to a defined version of the Standard as interpreted by The Forum.	The Certification Policy – in conjunction with the Conformance Requirements, Certification Agreement, and Trademark License Agreement – constitutes the set of requirements and obligations for achieving certification.
Conformance Statement	The document in which an organization declares its Scope of Certification.	The Scope of Certification as specified by the organization in the Conformance Statement Questionnaire will be the Scope of Certification that appears in the certificate and on the public registry when an organization is granted certification. The organization will also specify their tier of certification in the Conformance Statement Questionnaire.

Documents	Definition	Major Relevance
The Standard: The Open Trusted Technology Provider Standard (O-TTPS), Version 1.1 or ISO/IEC 20243:2015	An open standard containing a set of guidelines, requirements, and recommendations that help assure against maliciously tainted and counterfeit products throughout the COTS ICT product life cycle encompassing the following phases: design, sourcing, build, fulfillment, distribution, sustainment, and disposal.	The Standard was developed by The Forum and approved by The Open Group, through The Open Group Company Review consensus process. It was also approved by ISO/IEC as ISO/IEC 20243:2015. The two standards are technically equivalent. Chapter 4 of the Standard contains the requirements and recommendations. The requirements, for which conformance is mandatory within the Certification Program, are denoted as "shall" requirements within Chapter 4 of the Standard. They are also included in Appendix A of this Management Guide.
Trademark License Agreement (TMLA)	The agreement that contains the legal commitment by the organization to the conditions for use of the Certification Logo.	The TMLA will need to be signed by the organization and the Certification Authority, and the certification granted by the Certification Authority before the organization may use the Certification Logo in association with their declared Scope of Certification.

Chapter 5
Self-Assessed Certification Process

In the previous chapters we provided summary information on preparing for certification and beginning the process. This chapter covers the process for the Self-Assessed tier in more detail.

The O-TTPS Certification Program includes the following major phases for the Self-Assessed approach:
1. Preparing for certification
2. Performing the assessment
3. Registering for certification with the Certification Authority
4. Finalization by the Certification Authority

The major phases are described in Figure 2. Detailed flow charts are found in the Certification Policy.

Figure 2: The Self-Assessed Certification Process (Simplified)

5.1   Major Phases of Self-Assessed Certification

5.1.1   Phase 1: Preparing for Self-Assessed Certification
Chapter 3 of this Management Guide describes in general how to organize and prepare for the certification process. Chapter 4 provides a list of documents, which include further details of the process and the terms and conditions for certification. Both chapters should be reviewed for guidance and the documents listed in Chapter 4 should be read to assure you comprehend the commitment you are making, and the buy-in you will need to obtain from your organization.

5.1.2   Phase 2: Performing the Assessment within the Self-Assessed Tier
The organization must perform a self-assessment. It is recommended – but not mandated – that the assessment be performed using the Assessment Procedures because they provide excellent guidance and represent the global standard on how to assess conformance to the requirements in the Standard. In fact, while the Assessment Procedures are recommended for the Self-Assessed tier, they are mandated for the Third-Party Assessed tier.

While the assessment may be performed by the organization itself, it is permissible and worth considering for the organization to use a third party to help perform the assessment in the Self-Assessed tier. For example, O-TTPS Recognized Assessors may be able to assist the organization with this process.

The important fact to remember when considering the Self-Assessed approach is that by selecting this option, the organization is warranting that, to the best of its knowledge, it is conformant with the mandatory requirements of the Standard throughout the declared Scope of Certification. Accordingly, the need for due diligence in ascertaining and assuring conformance should not be overlooked.

In the Self-Assessed approach, when choosing the Scope of Certification, an organization is encouraged to look at all the products within that declared scope and all the processes that are used throughout the life cycle of all of the products within that scope, to determine if the applicable processes are implemented in conformance with the requirements in the Standard. If an organization identifies one or more products or product lines within the declared scope where there is a lack of conformance, the organization should either rectify the gaps, narrow the declared Scope of Certification, or identify the non-conformant products, product lines, or business units and declare them excluded from the Scope of Certification in the Conformance Statement Questionnaire. The modified Scope of Certification – explicitly omitting any exclusions – will be listed on the registry.

It is worth noting that the method for choosing a set of representative products in third-party assessments involves applying a set of Implementation Selection Criteria (ISC), developed by Carnegie Melon (i.e., location, supplier bases, types and complexity of technologies, governance structure, and customer base), to the Scope of Certification and using those to aide in identifying a set of products that is a representative sample of all of the products within that Scope of Certification. Application of those criteria to the declared scope helps assure that the products that are used to represent the scope, and ultimately to demonstrate conformance to the Standard, are truly representative of the global nature of the products, their components, their supply chains, and the various technologies that are within the scope.

In the Self-Assessed tier, although an organization is not *required* to apply the ISC to determine a set of products that is representative of their scope, it would still be valuable to identify and choose a set of products that represents a cross-section of the products within their scope and then assess conformance to the requirements in the Standard throughout that sample set of representative products. Alternatively, an organization might want to start by choosing a set of processes, and then determine whether those processes are conformant to the Standard. The organization will then determine which of the products within a product line, business unit, or the entire organization apply those processes consistently. This analysis will help the organization determine its Scope of Certification – whether for one or more products, a product line, a business unit, or the entire organization.

The advantage of choosing one or more selected representative products to assess conformance is that it provides a systematic approach to understanding what is expected to assert conformance. And while in the Self-Assessed approach it is not required that an organization present their evidence or their findings to become certified, it is recommended that an organization use the existing tools and templates, particularly the Assessment Procedures and the Certification Package Template (see the documents table for the Third-Party

Assessed tier in Chapter 6 of this Management Guide) and retain them in their internal records.

It is recommended that the organization who chooses the Self-Assessed approach retain the assessment records for the duration of the certification period because, in the event conformance is challenged after certification is granted, per Section 4.2 of the Certification Policy, those records will be very helpful to the organization in the requirement that they be able to substantiate the assertion of conformance made by the organization in the Certification Agreement.

5.1.3   Phase 3: Registering for Certification with the Certification Authority

Once Phase 2 is complete, then the organization may be ready to register with the Certification Authority. This phase includes:

- Signing the Certification Agreement
- Paying the Certification Fee
- Specifying the organization's Certification Contacts
- Submitting a completed Conformance Statement Questionnaire, which describes in detail the parameters of the certification, including the Scope of Certification, the tier of certification for which they are applying, and the nature of the organization as it pertains to their scope
- Signing the Trademark License Agreement

5.1.4   Phase 4: Finalization by the Certification Authority

In this phase the Certification Authority checks that the documentation received is in order and reviews the Conformance Statement for suitability and completeness.

Once the review is finished and if certification is awarded, the organization is:

- Notified in writing by the Certification Authority
- Listed on the public certification register by the Certification Authority
- Allowed to use the Certification Logo in accordance with the Trademark License Agreement

Chapter 6

Third-Party Assessed Certification Process

The Third-Party Assessed certification process includes the procedures for the certification process when a third-party O-TTPS Recognized Assessor is used. The major phases are described in Figure 3. Detailed flow charts are found in the Certification Policy.

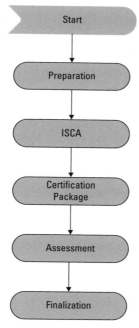

Figure 3: Simplified Third-Party Assessed Certification Process

6.1   Major Phases of the Third-Party Assessment

The O-TTPS Certification Program for the Third-Party Assessed tier includes five major phases:

1. Preparation for certification
2. Completing the Implementation Selection Criteria Application (ISCA) Document

3. Completing the Certification Package
4. Performing the third-party assessment
5. Validation and finalization by the Certification Authority

6.1.1 Phase 1: Preparing for Third-Party Assessed Certification

Phase 1 describes the preparation for certification that an organization will need to work on before embarking on formal certification. Chapter 3 of this Management Guide describes preparation in general; how to organize, solicit internal support, and choose an Assessor, etc. Chapter 4 of this Management Guide provides a list of documents, which include further details of the process and the terms and conditions for certification. Both chapters should be reviewed for guidance and the documents listed in Chapter 4 should be read to assure you comprehend the commitment you are making, and the buy-in you will need to obtain from your organization.

The relevant documents, which are *common to both* the Self-Assessed and the Third-Party Assessed approaches, are listed in Table 1 in Chapter 4. Additionally, the documents listed in Table 2 of this chapter are *required* for the Third-Party Assessed certification process.

It should be noted that it may be quite useful to reference and use the Assessment Procedures and the Certification Package Document (described below) for the Self-Assessed approach as well.

6.1.1.1 Selecting a Recognized Assessor

The organization must contract with an O-TTPS Recognized Assessor company to perform the third-party assessment. The organization chooses an O-TTPS Recognized Assessor from the registry of O-TTPS Recognized Assessors to perform its assessment and contracts independently with them to provide the assessment. This registry will be maintained on the Certification Authority's website. A current list of O-TTPS Recognized Assessors can be found on the public registry here: http://ottps-cert.opengroup.org/recognized-assessors.

To be recognized by The Open Group as an O-TTPS Recognized Assessor, a company must meet the criteria defined in the O-TTPS Recognized Assessor Agreement (an agreement between the Certification Authority and the O-TTPS Recognized Assessor), which can be found at http://ottps-cert.opengroup.org.

Table 2: Supporting Certification Documents (for Third-Party Assessed Tier)

Documents	Definition	Major Relevance
Assessment Procedures	This document specifies the procedures to be utilized by an Assessor when conducting a conformity assessment to the mandatory requirements in the Standard.	O-TTPS Recognized Assessors must use the Assessment Procedures when evaluating organizations that choose the Third-Party Assessed approach. Organizations applying for Third-Party Assessed certification will find the Assessment Procedures quite useful as the type of Evidence of Conformance that is required or recommended for each requirement in the Standard is specified in these procedures. Although organizations who choose the Self-Assessed approach are not required to use the Assessment Procedures for their assessments, they will likely find them very helpful in guiding their determination of conformance.
Certification Package Document	The document in which the organization defines the relationship between each requirement and the Evidence of Conformance; it is also where the Recognized Assessor subsequently records the assessment findings and provides the Assessment Report.	This is the document in which the organization provides pointers to the evidence that will be looked at by the Assessor, as specified in the Assessment Procedures.

Documents	Definition	Major Relevance
ISCA Document	The document in which the organization identifies a set of representative products from within the Scope of Certification and provides the methodology and rationale used in applying the Implementation Selection Criteria to make the selection. The Evidence of Conformance associated with the Selected Representative Products will be assessed against the Conformance Requirements.	Utilization of this document is required in the Third-Party Assessed approach. It will be completed and submitted by the organization to the Certification Authority. The Certification Authority will approve their proposed Scope of Certification and their set of Selected Representative Products.

The assessment fees, to be determined by the Recognized Assessor (company), will vary depending on the Scope of Certification, the variability of processes in the Scope of Certification, and the approved number of Selected Representative Products. The duration of the assessment will have the same dependencies and in addition will depend on how prepared the organization is going into the assessment.

The organization informs the Certification Authority on which O-TTPS Recognized Assessor has been engaged. Should the organization subsequently change its choice of O-TTPS Recognized Assessor, the organization must notify the Certification Authority of the change.

6.1.2   Phase 2: Completing the ISCA Document

Phase 2 is focused on identifying a set of products from within the Scope of Certification that is representative of all O-TTPS-related processes used in the Scope of Certification. This will be achieved through two steps:

- Mapping all of the O-TTPS processes used by the organization throughout the product life cycle of those Selected Representative Products to the requirements in the Standard
- Applying a defined set of Selection Criteria (i.e., location, supplier bases, types and complexity of technologies, governance structure, and customer base) to the Scope of Certification and identifying a set of products that

is a representative sample of all of the products from within that Scope of Certification

The resultant set of Selected Representative Products, approved by the Certification Authority, will be used during the assessment phase to assess the provider's conformance to the requirements. The mapping tables created during this phase help the organization to prepare their Certification Package in Phase 2.

Once an organization has determined their Scope of Certification, the organization must complete the ISCA Document per the instructions within the document to the satisfaction of the Certification Authority. The ISCA Document can be downloaded from the left-hand navigation bar on the Getting Started web page at http://ottps-cert.opengroup.org.

The objective of this activity is to identify a subset of products within the Scope of Certification that is representative of the Scope of Certification. All Selected Representative Products will be used for assessing the organization's conformance to the Conformance Requirements.

The ISCA Document also contains a description of the methodology and rationale used to apply the Implementation Selection Criteria in the selection and any other information that the organization may want to disclose to the Certification Authority to justify its Selected Representative Products.

The three major steps in completing the ISCA Document are listed below:
1. Describe the Scope of Certification.
   The organization selects and documents the Scope of Certification in the ISCA Document (refer to Section 2.1 in the ISCA Document).
2. Determine and draft the data for the ISCA Document.
   This step comprises two separate activities, which must be completed but may be performed in the order that most suits a specific organization and Scope of Certification:
   – Map processes to attributes and to Selected Representative Products: The organization identifies all of the O-TTPS processes that are employed within the Scope of Certification, and for which the organization is required to submit Evidence of Conformance. In order to complete this

activity, an organization must map every identified process to a Selected Representative Product in (see the Appendix of the ISCA Document).

– Apply ISC (identify Selected Representative Products): Based upon the Implementation Selection Criteria (ISC), the organization determines and documents the Selected Representative Products to be used to provide Evidence of Conformance within the Scope of Certification (see Appendix B of the ISCA Document). For an example of how to apply the ISC to your Scope of Certification, see Appendix C of the ISCA Document.

3. Finalize data in the completed ISCA Document and submit it to the Certification Authority.
The organization ensures the consistency of the activities in Step 2 and finalizes the data it has entered into the ISCA Document. When the organization is satisfied that the ISCA Document is complete and consistent, the organization submits it to the Certification Authority for approval. The Certification Authority must approve both the Conformance Statement, which includes the Scope of Certification, and the ISCA Document, which includes the Selected Representative Products, before the organization can move forward in the assessment process.

6.1.3 Phase 3: Completing the Certification Package

Phase 3 is focused on preparing the Certification Package. The organization assembles the Certification Package with Evidence of Conformance and pointers to the evidence for each of the requirements defined in the Standard, for each of the Selected Representative Products. This Certification Package is the basis for the assessment in Phase 4. Details on Phase 3 are available in the Certification Package Document.

The Certification Package Document can be downloaded from the left-hand navigation bar of the Getting Started web page at http://ottps-cert.opengroup.org. It contains the following:

- The Selected Representative Products table, which is taken from Appendix B of the ISCA Document once the organization has completed the ISCA Document and it has been approved by the Certification Authority.
- The Scope of Certification, which is taken from Section 2.1 of the ISCA Document, as aligned with the Conformance Statement.
- The Attribute to Process Mapping table, which is taken from Appendix A of the ISCA Document.

- The Evidence of Conformance tables, where the applicant provides pointers to the Evidence of Conformance submitted for each of the requirements defined in the Standard, and which the Recognized Assessor uses to record their findings.
- The Assessment Report Template to be completed by the Recognized Assessor prior to submission to the Certification Authority.

The primary activity for the organization in this phase is completing the Evidence of Conformance tables, which is described in detail in the Certification Package Document. There is one table for each requirement, which will need to be completed by the organization with supporting information, along with pointers to the Evidence of Conformance for that requirement.

It will be quite helpful for the organization to reference the Assessment Procedures as well during this activity, as there are certain types of evidence that are required or recommended for each O-TTPS requirement. As specified in the Assessment Procedures, there are two categories of requirements in the Standard and consequently two categories of evidence: process and implementation, as described below:

- Process evidence shows that established policies, processes. or procedures exist.
- Implementation evidence shows that the established processes have been applied to each of the Selected Representative Products.

The Assessment Procedures and the Certification Package Template specify what type of evidence is needed for each O-TTPS requirement.

Please see the Certification Package Template for further detail. More detailed instructions and an example of a completed Table of Conformance can be found in Section 3 of the Certification Package Template.

6.1.4   Phase 4: Performing the Third-Party Assessment

Phase 4 is focused on the assessment, during which an O-TTPS Recognized Assessor, contracted independently by the organization, assesses the Evidence of Conformance provided by the organization in the Certification Package to ensure that the organization conforms to the requirements defined in the Standard explicitly throughout the product life cycle of each of those Selected

Representative Products and implicitly throughout the entire Scope of
Certification.

The Recognized Assessor assesses the Certification Package Document and
the Evidence of Conformance it references. Applying the Assessment Procedures, the Recognized Assessor determines whether the evidence provided
demonstrates the organization's conformity to the Conformance Requirements
(i.e., each of the mandatory requirements in the Standard) for each of the
Selected Representative Products.

The Recognized Assessor records comments, regarding conformance to each
of the requirements, in the Certification Package Document according to the
instructions in the Assessment Procedures.

Once the Recognized Assessor has completed the Assessment Report and is able
to recommend certification to the Certification Authority, both the organization
and the Recognized Assessor review and sign the Assessment Report. The
Recognized Assessor submits the updated Certification Package Document,
including the Assessment Report, to the Certification Authority.

6.1.5   Phase 5: Validation and Finalization by the Certification Authority

The Certification Authority reviews the completed Certification Package
Document that was submitted by the Assessor for consistency and completeness
and to determine whether:

- The Certification Package Document is complete.
- The Assessment Report is unambiguous.
- The content and style are consistent with the Certification Package
  Documents from other O-TTPS certification applications.

If the Certification Authority believes the Assessor's findings are insufficient,
then the Certification Authority may require the Assessor to provide clarification or additional rationale to support the findings.

The Certification Authority will notify the organization in writing of the
outcome of the certification process. If the result is success, once the Trademark
License Agreement is in place, the Certification Authority will certify the

organization and list them on the public registry, which can be found here: http://ottps-cert.opengroup.org/certification-register.

The organization's obligations to remain conformant throughout the renewal period, which at the time of this writing is three (3) years, are contained in the Certification Policy and the Certification Agreement, which were signed by the organization and the Certification Authority at the beginning of the process. The organization's obligations on the use of the Trademark are contained in the Trademark License Agreement.

In the event there is a complaint that a certified Open Trusted Technology Provider is non-conformant during the certification period, there is an appeals process that is defined in the Certification Policy, which is managed by The Open Group. If an organization is in fact found to be non-conformant, then the organization will need to fix the non-conformity with a certain time period, or be taken off the public registry and the use of the Trademark revoked.

Chapter 7

Summary of the Certification Steps

They certification steps are listed here as a summary and can be found in more detail in the Certification Policy. Section 7.1 provides a summary of the steps for the Self-Assessed tier and Section 7.2 provides a summary of the steps for the Third-Party Assessed tier.

7.1   Certification Steps for Self-Assessed Tier

7.1.1   Preparation for Certification
Prior to registering for certification, with a goal of ensuring that it is ready for entry into the O-TTPS Certification Program, the organization should become familiar with the Referenced Documents and any other informative documents, such as FAQs.

Once an organization believes it is in conformance with the Conformance Requirements for the defined Scope of Certification, the organization may register for certification.

7.1.2   Organization Conducts Self-Assessment
The organization should conduct a self-assessment to determine whether, to the best of their knowledge, they are in conformance with the Standard throughout their Scope of Certification. This assessment may be conducted internally or externally by a third party, which could be an O-TTPS Recognized Assessor. Organizations undergoing self-assessment should use the published Assessment Procedures as guidance for determining conformance. Organizations conducting self-assessments should retain evidence and documentation that support their assertion of conformance.

7.1.3   Registering for Certification
The first step in the process is for the organization to register its intent to be certified by completing the registration information and submitting it along with the Certification Agreement and Certification Fee to the Certification Authority.

As part of the registration process, the organization must specify the organization's Certification Contacts.

All notifications regarding this certification and any subsequent renewals will be sent by the Certification Authority to the Certification Contacts. It is the responsibility of the organization to ensure that these Certification Contacts are kept up-to-date for the duration of the certification.

7.1.4   Completing the Conformance Statement Questionnaire

The organization must produce a Conformance Statement using the Conformance Statement Questionnaire. The Conformance Statement defines:
- The legal entity applying for certification
- The tier to which the legal entity is applying
- The version of the Standard to which the organization conforms
- The Scope of Certification for the proposed certification
- Optionally, any defined exclusions (e.g., products, product lines, geographies, etc.) that the organization would like explicitly listed as outside the Scope of Certification

The O-TTPS Certification Program allows the organization to choose its Scope of Certification. The organization will be certified for conforming to the Standard throughout a particular scope, which may be identified as one or more individual products, a product line or business unit, or an entire organization. Indicate the nature of the organization as it applies to the organization's Scope of Certification; for example, OEM, component supplier, value-add reseller, integrator, distributor.

7.1.5   Certification Authority Reviews the Conformance Statement

The Certification Authority reviews the completed Conformance Statement for consistency and completeness to determine whether:
- The Conformance Statement is complete.
- The content and style are consistent with the Conformance Statements from other O-TTPS certification applications.

The Certification Authority will respond to the organization within 20 days to provide approval or an explanation of any elements that need further clarification or revision in the Conformance Statement.

7.1.6   Organization Signs Trademark License Agreement

If the organization has not previously completed a Trademark License Agreement for use of the Certification Logo, it must be completed at this stage. The Certification Authority's website contains information on how to obtain and complete the Trademark License Agreement.

7.1.7   Certification Awarded

The Certification Authority will notify the organization in writing of the outcome of the certification process.

If the result is success and there is a Trademark License Agreement in place, the Certification Authority will certify the organization, issue the certificate, and enter the organization's details into the public certification registry. The organization will also be notified that the Certification Logo may then be used according to the terms defined in the Trademark License Agreement.

7.2   Certification Steps for Third-Party Assessed Tier

7.2.1   Preparation for Certification

Prior to registering for certification, with a goal of ensuring that it is ready for entry into the O-TTPS Certification Program, the organization should become familiar with the Referenced Documents and any other informative documents, such as FAQs.

Once an organization believes it is in conformance with the Conformance Requirements for the defined Scope of Certification, the organization may register for certification.

7.2.2   Registering for Certification

The first step in the process is for the organization to register its intent to be certified by completing the registration information and submitting it along with the Certification Agreement and Certification Fee to the Certification Authority.

As part of the registration process, the organization must specify the organization's Certification Contacts.

All notifications regarding this certification and any subsequent renewals will be sent by the Certification Authority to the Certification Contacts. It is the responsibility of the organization to ensure that these Certification Contacts are kept up-to-date for the duration of the certification.

7.2.3   Completing the Conformance Statement Questionnaire

The organization must produce a Conformance Statement using the Conformance Statement Questionnaire. The Conformance Statement defines:

- The legal entity applying for certification
- The version of the Standard to which the organization conforms
- The Scope of Certification for the proposed certification
- Optionally, any defined exclusions (e.g., products, product lines, geographies, etc.) that the organization would like explicitly listed as outside the Scope of Certification
- The nature of the organization as it applies to the organization's Scope of Certification (e.g., OEM, component supplier, value-add reseller, integrator, distributor)
- The name of the selected O-TTPS Recognized Assessor organization

The O-TTPS Certification Program allows the organization to choose its Scope of Certification. The organization will be certified for conforming to the Standard throughout a particular scope, which may be identified as one or more individual products, a product line or business unit, or an entire organization.

7.2.4   Completing the ISCA Document

The organization must complete the ISCA Document per the instructions within the document to the satisfaction of the Certification Authority. The objective of this activity is to identify a subset of products within the Scope of Certification that is representative of the Scope of Certification. All Selected Representative Products will be assessed for conformance to the Conformance Requirements.

The ISCA Document also contains a description of the methodology and rationale used to apply the Implementation Selection Criteria in the selection and any other information that the organization may want to disclose to the Certification Authority to justify its Selected Representative Products.

7.2.5   Certification Authority Reviews and Approves the Conformance Statement and ISCA Document

The Certification Authority will review the Conformance Statement and the ISCA Document. Since there may be considerable variation between applications for certification in both the Scope of Certification and the Selected Representative Products, the Certification Authority will also review these documents for consistency across other O-TTPS certification applications and for appropriate selection of products.

The Certification Authority will keep confidential and not share with the Assessor information related to how the organization applies the Implementation Selection Criteria and the methodology and rationale used to choose the Selected Representative Products.

The Certification Authority must approve both the Conformance Statement, which includes the Scope of Certification, and the ISCA Document, which includes the Selected Representative Products, before the organization can move forward in the Assessment process. The Certification Authority will respond to the organization within 20 days to provide approval or an explanation of any elements that need further clarification or revision in the Conformance Statement or the ISCA Document.

7.2.6   Organization Selects an O-TTPS Recognized Assessor

The organization chooses an O-TTPS Recognized Assessor from the registry of O-TTPS Recognized Assessors to perform its assessment. This registry will be maintained on the Certification Authority's website.

To be recognized by The Open Group as an O-TTPS Recognized Assessor, a company must meet the criteria defined in the O-TTPS Recognized Assessor Agreement. The company must also enter into the O-TTPS Recognized Assessor Agreement with the Certification Authority. The rationale and process for removing an O-TTPS Recognized Assessor from the registry of O-TTPS Recognized Assessors is defined in the O-TTPS Recognized Assessor Agreement.

The organization informs the Certification Authority which O-TTPS Recognized Assessor has been engaged. Should the organization subsequently change its choice of O-TTPS Recognized Assessor, the organization must notify the Certification Authority.

7.2.7   Organization Prepares Certification Package

After the Certification Authority approves the Selected Representative Products, the organization assembles the Certification Package, which consists of the Certification Package Document and the Evidence of Conformance. The Certification Package Document contains a table for each requirement in which the organization must supply pointers to evidence that demonstrates conformance to that requirement for every Selected Representative Product. The Evidence of Conformance is all material referenced in the Certification Package Document and necessary to demonstrate conformance to the Conformance Requirements. The organization submits the Certification Package to the Assessor.

7.2.8   Assessor Performs the Assessment

The Assessor assesses the Certification Package Document and the Evidence of Conformance it references. Applying the Assessment Procedures, the Assessor determines whether the evidence provided demonstrates the organization's conformity to the Conformance Requirements for each of the Selected Representative Products.

The Assessor records comments regarding conformance to the Conformance Requirements in the Certification Package Document according to the instructions in the Assessment Procedures.

For an assessment for initial certification, there is no time limit for the assessment to complete. In the case of re-certification, the assessment must complete within the timeframe defined in Section 8.2 of the Certification Policy.

7.2.9   Assessor Recommends Certification

Once the Assessor has completed the Assessment Report and is able to recommend certification, both the organization and the Assessor review and sign the Assessment Report. The Assessor submits the updated Certification Package Document, including the Assessment Report, to the Certification Authority.

This fully complete Certification Package Document forms the Certification Authority's record of the assessment.

The Evidence of Conformance that was submitted to the Assessor remains with the Assessor and must be archived for a period of at least six (6) years.

7.2.10 Certification Authority Reviews the Certification Package Document

The Certification Authority reviews the completed Certification Package Document for consistency and completeness and to determine whether:

- The Certification Package Document is complete.
- The Assessment Report is unambiguous.
- The content and style are consistent with the Certification Package Documents from other O-TTPS certification applications.

If the Certification Authority believes the Assessor's findings are insufficient, then the Certification Authority may require the Assessor to provide clarification or additional rationale to support the findings.

7.2.11 Organization Signs Trademark License Agreement

If the organization has not previously completed a Trademark License Agreement for use of the Certification Logo, it must be completed at this stage. The Certification Authority's website contains information on how to obtain and complete the Trademark License Agreement.

7.2.12 Certification Awarded

The Certification Authority will notify the organization in writing of the outcome of the certification process.

If the result is success and there is a Trademark License Agreement in place, the Certification Authority will certify the organization, issue the certificate, and enter the organization's details into the public certification registry.

The organization will also be notified that the Certification Logo may then be used according to the terms defined in the Trademark License Agreement.

O-TTPS Requirements

A.1   Introduction

This Appendix, excluding this Introduction section, is taken verbatim from the Terminology section (Section 1.4) of the Standard (i.e., O-TTPS Version 1.1, which is technically equivalent to ISO/IEC 20243:2015). It defines the prescriptive terms used in Chapter 4 of the Standard, which defines the requirements and recommendations for mitigating the risk of tainted and counterfeit products.

Note: The terminology and the recommendations and requirements of the current version of the Standard – which at the time of this writing can be found here: www.opengroup.org/bookstore/catalog/c147.htm – take precedence over the requirements extracted in this Appendix.

A.2   Terminology

The terminology below, which can be found in Section 1.4 of the Standard, provides a set of terms and their definitions, which should be used when describing and interpreting the Standard requirements and recommendations specified in this section. These terms are aligned with ISO/IEC Directives, Part 2 (Annex H).

Shall   Indicates an absolute, mandatory requirement of the Standard that has to be implemented in order to conform to the Standard and from which no deviation is permitted. Do not use "must" as an alternative for "shall". (This will avoid any confusion between the requirements of a document and external statutory obligations.)

Shall not   Indicates an absolute preclusion of the Standard, and if implemented would represent a non-conformity with the Standard. Do not use "may not" instead of "shall not" to express a prohibition.

Should   Indicates a recommendation among several possibilities that is
                  particularly suitable, without mentioning or excluding others,
                  or that a certain course of action is preferred but not necessarily
                  required.

Should not   Indicates a practice explicitly recommended not to be
                  implemented, or that a certain possibility or course of action is
                  deprecated but not prohibited. To conform to the Standard, an
                  acceptable justification must be presented if the requirement is
                  implemented.

May   Indicates an optional requirement to be implemented at the
                  discretion of the practitioner. Do not use "can" instead of "may" in
                  this context.

Can   Used for statements of possibility and capability, whether material,
                  physical, or causal.

A.3   Requirements and Recommendations

This Standard is described in terms of the provider's product life cycle. The
collection of provider best practices contained in the Standard are those that
the Forum considers best capable of influencing and governing the integrity of
a COTS ICT product from its inception to proper disposal at end-of-life. These
provider practices are divided into two basic categories of product life cycle
activities as described: Technology Development and Supply Chain Security:

- The provider's Technology Development activities for a COTS ICT product
  are mostly under the provider's in-house supervision in how they are
  executed. The methodology areas that are most relevant to assuring against
  tainted and counterfeit products are: Product Development/Engineering
  methods and Secure Development/Engineering methods.
- The provider's Supply Chain Security activities focus on best practices where
  the provider must interact with third parties who produce their agreed
  contribution with respect to the product's life cycle. Here, the provider's best
  practices often control the point of intersection with the outside supplier
  through control points that may include inspection, verification, and
  contracts.

While these categories are useful as an organizing construct, they are not absolute distinctions; for example, one product may be handled by the provider's own organization exclusively, while another product's life cycle could involve many aspects being handled in conjunction with a variety of third parties as governed by the provider. These two major categories of the product life cycle are depicted in Figure 4:

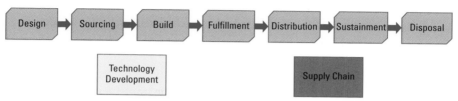

Figure 4: Product Life Cycle – Categories and Activities

For structural purposes, the requirements and recommendations are delineated in separate sections according to which of the two major categories they fit into – Technology Development and Supply Chain Security. However, from an operational perspective, there is some overlap between best practices that might be followed in-house during Technology Development, and those that might be invoked between a supplier and a provider at a particular interface in the Supply Chain. The shading in the diagram above depicts an example of this overlap of boundaries.

The following sections include the prescriptive requirements and recommendations for the Standard. The requirements are focused on the two identified threats. Some are highly correlated to the specific threats; others are more foundational but considered essential.

A.4   Technology Development

For purposes of addressing tainted and counterfeit products, the Technology Development category of the product life cycle reflects the following methods, which are referred to in Section 4.1 and Section 4.2 of the Standard.

1. Product Development/Engineering Method (PD): Trusted Technology Providers use a well-defined, documented, and repeatable product development or engineering method and/or process. The effectiveness of the method is managed through metrics and management oversight.

2. Secure Development/Engineering Method (SE): Trusted Technology Providers employ a secure engineering method when designing and developing their products. Software providers and suppliers often employ methods or processes with the objective of identifying, detecting, fixing, and mitigating defects and vulnerabilities that could be exploited, as well as verifying the security and resiliency of the finished products. Hardware providers and suppliers also include ways to mitigate use of unverified and inauthentic software and to protect against counterfeit hardware or software.

A.4.1   PD: Product Development/Engineering Method

The following sections contain the best practice requirements and recommendations primarily associated with the Technology Development category of activities relating to the product development/engineering method.

PD_DES: Software/Firmware/Hardware Design Process

Attribute Definition

A formal process exists that defines and documents how requirements are translated into a product design.

Requirements

PD_DES.01	A process shall exist that assures the requirements are addressed in the design.
PD_DES.02	Product requirements shall be documented.
PD_DES.03	Product requirements should be tracked as part of the design process.

PD_CFM: Configuration Management

Attribute Definition

A formal process and supporting systems exist which assure the proper management, control, and tracking of change to product development and manufacturing assets and artifacts.

Requirements

PD_CFM.01	A documented formal process shall exist which defines the configuration management process and practices.
PD_CFM.02	Baselines of identified assets and artifacts under configuration management shall be established.
PD_CFM.03	Changes to identified assets and artifacts under configuration management shall be tracked and controlled.
PD_CFM.04	Configuration management should be applied to build management and development environments used in the development/ engineering of the product.
PD_CFM.05	Access to identified assets and artifacts and supporting systems shall be protected and secured.
PD_CFM.06	A formal process shall exist that establishes acceptance criteria for work products accepted into the product baseline.

PD_MPP: Well-defined Development/Engineering Method Process and Practices

Attribute Definition
Development/engineering processes and practices are documented, and managed and followed across the life cycle.

Requirements

PD_MPP.01	The development/engineering process as documented should be inclusive of development partners as defined by the governance process.
PD_MPP.02	The development/engineering process shall be able to track, as appropriate, components that are proven to be targets of tainting or counterfeiting as they progress through the life cycle.

PD_QAT: Quality and Test Management

Attribute Definition
Quality and test management is practiced as part of the product development/ engineering life cycle.

Requirements

PD_QAT.01	There shall be a quality and test product plan that includes quality metrics and acceptance criteria.
PD_QAT.02	Testing and quality assurance activities shall be conducted according to the plan.
PD_QAT.03	Products or components shall meet appropriate quality criteria throughout the life cycle.

PD_PSM: Product Sustainment Management

Attribute Definition
Product support, release maintenance, and defect management are product sustainment services offered to acquirers while the product is generally available.

Requirements

PD_PSM.01	A release maintenance process shall be implemented.
PD_PSM.02	Release maintenance shall include a process for notification to acquirers of product updates.
PD_PSM.03	Release maintenance shall include a product update process, which uses security mechanisms.
PD_PSM.04	A defect management process shall be implemented.
PD_PSM.05	The defect management process shall include: a documented feedback and problem reporting process.

A.4.2 SE: Secure Development/Engineering Method
The following sections contain the best practice requirements and recommendations primarily associated with the Technology Development category of activities relating to the secure development/engineering method.

SE_TAM: Threat Analysis and Mitigation

Attribute Definition
Threat analysis and mitigation identify a set of potential attacks on a particular product or system and describe how those attacks might be perpetrated and the best methods of preventing or mitigating potential attacks.

Requirements

SE_TAM.01	Product architecture and design shall be assessed against potential attacks to gain an understanding of the threat landscape.
SE_TAM.02	Threat mitigation strategies for tainted and counterfeit products shall be implemented as part of product development.
SE_TAM.03	Threat analysis shall be used as input to the creation of test plans and cases.

SE_RTP: Run-time Protection Techniques

Attribute Definition

Run-time protection techniques are considered part of a secure development/ engineering method. This includes techniques to mitigate the exploitation of vulnerabilities. For example, run-time protection techniques help defend executable code against buffer overflow attacks, null pointers, etc.

Requirements

SE_RTP.01	Run-time protection techniques as applicable to product architecture should be employed.
SE_RTP.02	Run-time protection techniques should be included to mitigate the impact of vulnerabilities.
SE_RTP.03	Run-time protection techniques should be included to protect executable code against memory space, buffer overflow attacks, and null pointers.

SE_VAR: Vulnerability Analysis and Response

Attribute Definition

Vulnerability analysis is the process of determining whether a product contains vulnerabilities and categorizing their potential severity.

Requirements

SE_VAR.01	Techniques and practices for vulnerability analysis shall be utilized. Some techniques include: code review, static analysis, penetration testing, white/black box testing, etc.
SE_VAR.02	The impact of published vulnerabilities to products and processes should be analyzed and mitigated.
SE_VAR.03	A process shall exist for governing notification of newly discovered and exploitable product vulnerabilities.
SE_VAR.04	Vulnerability analysis and response should feed into the processes for ongoing product development, product patching, and remediation.

SE_PPR: Product Patching and Remediation

Attribute Definition
A well-documented process exists for patching and remediating products. Priority is given to known severe vulnerabilities.

Requirements

SE_PPR.01	There shall be a well-documented process for patching and remediating products.
SE_PPR.02	There should be a process for informing an acquirer of notification and remediation mechanisms.
SE_PPR.03	Remediation of vulnerabilities shall be prioritized based on a variety of factors, including risk.
SE_PPR.04	Documented development and sustainment practices should be followed when implementing product remediation.

SE_SEP: Secure Engineering Practices

Attribute Definition
Secure engineering practices are established to avoid common engineering errors that lead to exploitable product vulnerabilities.

Requirements

SE_SEP.01	Secure coding practices shall be utilized to avoid common coding errors that lead to exploitable product vulnerabilities. For example, user input validation, use of appropriate compiler flags, etc.
SE_SEP.02	Secure hardware design practices (where applicable) shall be employed. For example, zeroing out memory and effective opacity.
SE_SEP.03	Training on secure engineering practices shall be provided to the appropriate personnel on a regular basis consistent with changing practices and the threat landscape.

SE_MTL: Monitor and Assess the Impact of Changes in the Threat Landscape

Attribute Definition
The threat landscape is monitored and the potential impacts of changes in the threat landscape are assessed on development/engineering practices, tools, and techniques.

Requirements

SE_MTL.01	Changes to the threat landscape should be monitored by periodically reviewing industry security alerts/bulletins.
SE_MTL.02	Changes to the development/engineering practices, tools, and techniques shall be assessed in light of changes to the threat landscape.
SE_MTL.03	The cause of product vulnerabilities shall be evaluated and appropriate changes to the development/engineering practices, tools, and techniques identified to mitigate similar vulnerabilities in the future.

A.5   Supply Chain Security

Trusted Technology Providers manage their supply chains through the application of defined, monitored, and validated supply chain processes. These processes, embodied in best practice requirements and recommendations, seek to ensure the security of the supply chain throughout the life cycle. In general, a technology supply chain attack is an attempt to disrupt the creation of goods by subverting the hardware, software, or configuration of a commercial product, prior to customer delivery (e.g., manufacturing, ordering, or distribution) for the purpose of introducing an exploitable vulnerability or perpetrating fraud through counterfeiting. The primary focus of the supply chain category of provider activities is to assure the integrity of the technology manufacturing/ development and support processes. This is the second product life cycle category used to organize the requirements in the Standard.

A.5.1 SC: Supply Chain Security

The following sections contain the best practice requirements and recommendations primarily associated with the Supply Chain Security category of activities relating to the product life cycle.

SC_RSM: Risk Management

Attribute Definition

The management of supply chain risk around tainted and counterfeit components and products includes the identification, assessment, prioritization, and mitigation of corresponding business, technical, and operational risks.

Requirements

SC_RSM.01	Changes to the threat landscape should be monitored by periodically reviewing industry security alerts/bulletins.
SC_RSM.02	Supply chain risk identification, assessment, prioritization, and mitigation shall be conducted.
SC_RSM.03	The output of risk identification, assessment, and prioritization shall be addressed by a mitigation plan, which shall be documented.
SC_RSM.04	The output of risk identification, assessment, and prioritization shall be addressed by a mitigation plan, which shall be followed routinely.
SC_RSM.05	The mitigation plan should be reviewed periodically by practitioners, including management, and revised as appropriate.
SC_RSM.06	Supply chain risk management training shall be incorporated in a provider's organizational training plan, which shall be reviewed periodically and updated as appropriate.

SC_PHS: Physical Security

Attribute Definition
Physical security procedures are necessary to protect development assets and artifacts, manufacturing processes, the plant floor, and the supply chain.

Requirements

SC_PHS.01	Risk-based procedures for physical security shall be established and documented.
SC_PHS.02	Risk-based procedures for physical security shall be followed routinely.
SC_PHS.03	Risk-based procedures for physical security should be reviewed periodically by practitioners, including management, and revised as appropriate.

SC_ACC: Access Controls

Attribute Definition
Proper access controls are established for the protection of product-relevant intellectual property against the introduction of tainted and counterfeit components where applicable in the supply chain. Access controls can vary by type of intellectual property and over time, during the life cycle.

Requirements

SC_ACC.01	Access controls shall be established and managed for product-relevant intellectual property, assets, and artifacts. Assets and artifacts include controlled elements related to the development/manufacturing of a provider's product.
SC_ACC.02	Access controls established and managed for product-relevant intellectual property, assets, and artifacts shall be documented.
SC_ACC.03	Access controls established and managed for product-relevant intellectual property, assets, and artifacts shall be followed routinely.

SC_ACC.04	Access controls established and managed for product-relevant intellectual property, assets, and artifacts should be reviewed periodically by practitioners, including management, and revised as appropriate.
SC_ACC.05	Access controls established and managed for product-relevant intellectual property, assets, and artifacts shall employ the use of access control auditing.

SC_ESS: Employee and Supplier Security and Integrity

Attribute Definition

Background checks are conducted for employees and contractors whose activities are directly related to sensitive product supply chain activities.

A Provider has a set of applicable business conduct guidelines for their employee and supplier communities.

A Provider obtains periodic confirmation that suppliers are conducting business in a manner consistent with principles embodied in industry conduct codes, such as the Electronic Industry Citizenship Coalition (EICC) Code of Conduct.

Requirements

SC_ESS.01	Proof of identity shall be ascertained for all new employees and contractors engaged in the supply chain, except where prohibited by law.
SC_ESS.02	Background checks should be conducted for employees and contractors whose activities are directly related to sensitive product supply chain activities (within reason given local customs and according to local law).
SC_ESS.03	A set of business conduct guidelines applicable to its employees and contractors should exist, consistent with principles embodied in industry conduct codes such as the Electronic Industry Citizenship Coalition (EICC) Code of Conduct.

SC_ESS.04	Business should be conducted in a manner consistent with principles embodied in industry conduct codes, such as the Electronic Industry Citizenship Coalition (EICC) Code of Conduct.
SC_ESS.05	Periodic confirmation that suppliers are conducting business in a manner consistent with principles embodied in industry conduct codes, such as the Electronic Industry Citizenship Coalition (EICC) Code of Conduct, should be obtained.

SC_BPS: Business Partner Security

(This includes, for example, Suppliers, Integrators, Logistic Partners, Channel Partners, and Authorized Resellers.)

Attribute Definition

Relevant business partners follow the recommended supply chain security best practice requirements specified by The Standard.

Periodic confirmation is requested that business partners are following the supply chain security best practices requirements specified by The Standard.

Requirements

SC_BPS.01	Supply chain security best practices (e.g., O-TTPS) shall be recommended to relevant business partners.
SC_BPS.02	Legal agreements with business partners should reference applicable requirements for supply chain security practices (e.g., O-TTPS).
SC_BPS.03	The provider should periodically request confirmation that business partners are following the supply chain security best practice requirements specified by the O-TTPS.

SC_STR: Supply Chain Security Training

Attribute Definition

Personnel responsible for the security of supply chain aspects are properly trained.

Requirements

SC_STR.01	Training in supply chain security procedures shall be given to all appropriate personnel.

SC_ISS: Information Systems Security

Attribute Definition

Supply Chain information systems properly protect data through an appropriate set of security controls.

Requirements

SC_ISS.01	Supply chain data shall be protected through an appropriate set of security controls.

SC_TTC: Trusted Technology Components

Attribute Definition

Supplied components are evaluated to assure that they meet component specification requirements.

Suppliers follow supply chain security best practices with regard to supplied components (e.g., O-TTPS).

Requirements

SC_TTC.01	The quality of supplied components shall be assessed against the component specification requirements.
SC_TTC.02	Counterfeit components shall not knowingly be incorporated into products.
SC_TTC.03	Suppliers should be required to follow supply chain security best practices with regard to supplied components (e.g. O-TTPS).
SC_TTC.04	Vulnerability responses to affected supplied components should be jointly managed with the supplier.

SC_STH: Secure Transmission and Handling

Attribute Definition

Secure transmission and handling of assets and artifacts during delivery is needed to lower the risk of product tampering while in transit to their destination.

Requirements

SC_STH.01	Secure transmission and handling controls shall be established and documented.
SC_STH.02	Secure transmission and handling controls shall be designed to lower the risk of physical tampering with assets and artifacts that are physically transported.
SC_STH.03	Secure transmission and handling controls shall be designed to lower the risk of tampering with assets and artifacts that are electronically transmitted.
SC_STH.04	Secure transmission and handling controls shall be followed routinely.
SC_STH.05	Secure transmission and handling controls should be reviewed periodically by practitioners, including management, and revised as appropriate.
SC_STH.06	For assets and artifacts and related information that are considered to be high risk from the supply chain perspective, additional countermeasures, such as authenticity verification, should be employed.
SC_STH.07	Methods of verifying authenticity and integrity of products after delivery should be available.

SC_OSH: Open Source Handling

Attribute Definition

Open Source components are managed as defined by the best practices within the O-TTPS for Product Development/ Engineering methods and Secure Development/Engineering methods.

Requirements

SC_OSH.01	Open Source assets and artifacts should be managed as defined by the best practices within the O-TTPS for Product Development/ Engineering methods and Secure Development/Engineering methods.
SC_OSH.02	In the management of Open Source assets and artifacts, components sourced shall be identified as derived from well-understood component lineage.
SC_OSH.03	In the management of Open Source assets and artifacts, components sourced shall be subject to well-defined acceptance procedures that include asset and artifact security and integrity before their use within a product.
SC_OSH.04	For such sourced components, responsibilities for ongoing support and patching shall be clearly understood.

SC_CTM: Counterfeit Mitigation

Attribute Definition
Practices are deployed to manufacture, deliver, and service products that do not contain counterfeit components.

Practices are deployed to control the unauthorized use of scrap from the hardware manufacturing process.

Requirements

SC_CTM.01	Instances of counterfeit activity relating to products shall be reviewed and an appropriate response sent.
SC_CTM.02	Proper disposal procedures upon end of life should be employed (e.g., clearing data from hard drives, rendering a PCB non-functional, etc.) to protect from re-use in counterfeit product.
SC_CTM.03	Practices should be deployed to preclude the unauthorized (counter-indicated) use of scrap from the hardware manufacturing process.
SC_CTM.04	Techniques shall be utilized as applicable and appropriate to mitigate the risk of counterfeiting, such as security labeling and scrap management techniques.

SC_MAL: Malware Detection

Attribute Definition

Practices are employed that mitigate as much as practical the inclusion of malware in components received from suppliers and components or products delivered to customers or integrators.

Requirements

SC_MAL.01	One or more up-to-date malware detection tools shall be deployed as part of the code acceptance and development processes.
SC_MAL.02	Malware detection techniques shall be used before final packaging and delivery (e.g., scanning finished products and components for malware using one or more up-to-date malware detection tools).

Appendix B

Additional Resources

This Appendix contains additional resources and references that provide useful information about the Forum, the O-TTPS, the O-TTPS Certification Program, and the Forum's other deliverables.

For additional O-TTPS resources, including recorded webinars, white papers, and mapping guides to other related standards, go to: www.opengroup.org/bookstore/catalog, and under the Titles by Subject section, click on Trusted Technology. They are freely available, but you will be asked to create an account or to log in with your existing account to obtain downloads.

B.1 Frequently Asked Questions

A set of Frequently Asked Questions about the O-TTPS Certification Program is available from the O-TTPS Certification website (http://ottps-cert.opengroup.org).

Note that this file may also be accessed from the left-hand navigation bar on the Getting Started web page at http://ottps-cert.opengroup.org.

B.2 Case Study

The IBM Case Study on The Open Group Accreditation as an Open Trusted Technology Provider™ is available at: www.opengroup.org/bookstore/catalog/y150.htm.

Index